The King and His Kingdom:
Devotions for Kids from the Parables of Jesus

Author Deborah A. Ellison
Illustrator Dave O'Connell

I0233934

Author: Deborah A. Ellison
Illustrator: Dave O'Connell

ISBN: 978-1-966382-02-7

Juvenile/NonFiction/Religion/Bible Stories/New Testament
Juvenile/NonFiction/Religious/Christian/Devotional & Prayer

EABooks Publishing
Your Partner In Publishing

Published by EA Books Publishing, a division of
Living Parables of Central Florida, Inc. a 501c3
EABooksPublishing.com

"Jesus was a master storyteller, but His stories were not just for the people of His day. Jesus' stories (called parables) give us a deeper understanding of His heavenly Kingdom and how we can become part of His Kingdom. In this wonderful devotional for families, Deborah Ellison features more than two dozen parables to help readers apply biblical truth to their everyday lives.

If you want to dig deeper into God's word and learn from the Master Storyteller, the devotions in this book will provide hours of meaningful moments as you and your children discover hidden truths in the parables of Jesus."

Crystal Bowman, bestselling, award-winning author of more than 100 books for children and families including Our Daily Bread for Kids—365 Devotions from Genesis to Revelation

What is a Parable?

Did you know that Jesus loved to tell stories? He told short stories called parables to teach important lessons about God's Kingdom and how we should live. These stories helped people understand what He wanted to say. Jesus also told stories to help people remember what He taught so they would obey His words.

A long time ago, people didn't have the kind of pens, pencils, or books we have today. Instead of books, they wrote on scrolls, which were long pieces of paper made from plants or animal skins. They would roll the scrolls up to keep them safe. But scrolls cost so much money that only special people like teachers and leaders used them. Because of this, most people learned by listening. They had to remember Jesus' words in their minds, and stories were easier to remember.

Let's check out some of the stories Jesus told and find out what we can learn from them!

The Unfair Judge

Scripture
Luke 18:1—8

Why should we keep praying? Jesus answers this question in a story:

Long ago, a judge lived in a city. People would come to him for help. He would listen to their problems, but he didn't really care about them, and he didn't love God.

One day, a woman came to see the judge. She said to him, "Please help me! Someone is being mean to me." At first the judge didn't pay attention to her, but the woman kept coming back to him. "Please help me!" she said again and again. "Someone is being mean to me."

The judge said to himself, "This woman is driving me crazy! I don't care about her problem, but I will help her because she keeps asking me."

So, the judge made a fair decision and helped the woman with her problem.

Jesus told this story to help us understand prayer. He wants us to know that we can always pray to God and never give up. God is the Judge who is always fair, and He cares about us. He is patient and will help people who need His help.

Main Point

Don't give up. Trust God and keep praying.

Take Action

1. **Why is it important to pray every day?**
2. **Who can you pray for today that needs God's help?**

The Foolish Rich Man

Scripture
Luke 12:16—21

One day, a man came to Jesus. His father had died, and he and his brother were fighting over the things their father had left behind. The man said to Jesus, "Please tell my brother to share our father's property with me."

Jesus knew the man was being greedy. Jesus told him that caring too much about money and the things he owned would turn his heart away from God.

Jesus told him a story about a rich man who grew so many fruits and vegetables on his farm that he didn't have enough room to store the food. So, he built bigger barns to store the food instead of sharing it with others. The man was very greedy. He decided to eat, drink, and enjoy everything he had for himself. He only thought about getting more things to fill his barns. The man loved his food and barns more than he loved God or people.

Main Point

Greed will turn your heart away from God.

Take Action

1. Why is it bad to be greedy?
2. What are some ways you can share with others?

Lazarus and the Rich Man

Scripture
Luke 16:19—31

Jesus wanted his followers to help people who were poor. He told the story of a rich man who had a lot of money. The rich man lived in a big, beautiful house. He wore nice clothes and had lots of food. He had more than he needed. Outside his gate was a poor man named Lazarus who was hungry and so sick that the dogs licked his sores. Lazarus wished he could just have the crumbs that fell from the rich man's table. But the rich man wouldn't share anything with him.

One day Lazarus died and was carried by angels to a good place called Heaven. The rich man also died and went to a sad place called Hades. Hades was filled with fire and was hotter than we can imagine. From far away, the rich man saw Abraham, a man who loved God and had lived a long time ago. Lazarus was at his side.

The rich man shouted, "Father Abraham, have pity on me! Send Lazarus to dip the tip of his finger in water and cool my tongue. I'm hurting in these flames."

But Abraham said, "Remember, when you were alive, you only thought about yourself and didn't help Lazarus. Now you are in Hades and Lazarus is in Heaven. No one can cross the big gap between us."

The rich man begged, "Please send Lazarus to my five brothers to tell them about this place so they don't end up here."

But Abraham replied, "They can read the Bible to learn how to turn away from doing bad things. They can turn to God so they don't end up in the sad place away from God."

Main Point

You can go to Heaven if you believe in Jesus as your Savior.

Take Action

1. Why should we help people who don't have money for food or clothes?
2. Share a treat with a friend or neighbor.

The Hidden Treasure

Scripture
Matthew 13:44

Have you ever found a treasure? Jesus told a story about a man who found a treasure in a hidden field. The man was so happy and excited to find the treasure that he hid it again to keep it safe. Then the man decided to sell everything he owned so that he could go back and buy the field. Now, the field and the treasure belonged to him forever! The man knew that he had something very special and valuable.

Jesus said that the Kingdom of Heaven is like having a treasure that lasts forever. It is more valuable than anything else in this world. You can have this treasure and belong to the Kingdom of Heaven when you believe in Jesus.

Main Point

The Kingdom of Heaven is like finding something special and valuable, like a treasure.

Take Action

1. Learn more about God by listening to Bible stories.
2. Think of two good things God has done for you and thank Him for that.

The Workers in the Garden

Scripture
Matthew 20:1—16

Jesus wanted His followers to understand that God's love is the same for everyone, so he told them this story:

A man owned a big garden, and he needed workers to take care of it. In the morning, he found workers and said, "Come and help in my garden. I will pay you at the end of the day."

At noon the man went into town and got more workers. He did the same at three o'clock and five o'clock in the afternoon.

At the end of the day, when it was time to pay the workers, he paid everyone the same amount of money, no matter how long they had worked in the garden. The workers who had been there longer thought they should receive more money.

The man who owned the garden explained, "I wanted to be kind to everyone—those who worked all day, and those who were only here for an hour. I can do what I want with my money. Don't be upset because I am kind to others."

Main Point

God gives His love and saves everyone who believes in Him, no matter when they become His children.

Take Action

1. Include every one of your playmates in your games, even if someone joins late.
2. Remember to say "thank you" to everyone who helps you, even if they only help a little bit.

The Pharisee and the Tax Collector

Scripture
Luke 18:9—14

Do you know someone who thinks they are better than everyone else? Jesus told a story to some people who thought they always did what was right. They also thought they were better than others. Jesus wanted to teach them an important lesson.

One day, two men went to the Temple to pray to God. One man was called a Pharisee, and he thought he was a very good person. The other man was a tax collector, and people didn't like him.

The Pharisee stood by himself and prayed out loud, "Thank you, God, that I am not like other people. I don't cheat or do anything wrong. I'm not like that tax collector over there! I always pray and give money to You."

But the tax collector felt sorry for the wrong things he had done. He didn't even look up to Heaven as he prayed; he just beat his chest in sadness and cried out, "God, please have mercy on me. I am a sinner!"

Then Jesus said that the tax collector, who didn't think he was better than others and was sorry for his sins, was the one who pleased God. The Pharisee, who thought he did everything right and thought he was better than others, didn't please God.

Main Point

Don't act like you are better than others or say mean things about them.

Take Action

1. Say something kind about each person in your family.
2. Say "I'm sorry" when you have done something wrong.

The Unforgiving Servant

Scripture
Matthew 18:23—35

Do you know that if we want to be more like Jesus, we need to forgive others? One day, while listening to Jesus, a man asked, "How many times should I forgive someone who is mean to me?" To help him understand, Jesus told this story:

A king had many servants who owed him money, so he decided to collect all the money. One servant owed him millions of dollars. The king asked the servant for the money he owed and became upset when the servant couldn't pay. Then the king said to the servant, "Everything you own must be sold to pay back my money."

The servant became very sad and begged the king, "Please give me more time, and I will pay it all." The king felt sorry for the servant and forgot about the money he owed and let him go.

After that, the servant who didn't have to pay the king went out and met another servant who owed him a much smaller amount. The forgiven servant wasn't kind like the king. He grabbed the other servant and said, "You must pay me now!"

The other servant begged for more time to pay back what he owed. But the forgiven servant had the other servant put in jail.

When the king heard about this, he was mad. He said to his servant, "I forgave you a big amount of money, but you couldn't forgive a small one. That's not right." Then the king sent the forgiven servant to jail because he was mean to another servant.

Main Point **Jesus forgives us when we do something wrong. If we want to be more like Jesus, we must forgive others too.**

Take Action

1. **What does it mean to forgive someone?**
2. **How can you show kindness to someone who has been mean to you?**

The Good Samaritan

Scripture
Luke 10:30 — 37

Do you know what it means to be a good neighbor? Jesus shared this story with a man who was trying to prove that he loved everyone:

A man was traveling from a city called Jerusalem to another place called Jericho. But on the way, some mean robbers hurt him badly. They took his clothes, beat him, and left him alone on the road.

After a while, a priest walked by. But the priest didn't stop to help the man. He crossed over to the other side of the road and kept walking.

Then, a Levite, who helped in the Temple, came by. He saw the hurt man, but crossed over to the other side of the road. And just like the priest, he kept walking.

What do you think happened next?

A Samaritan, whom some people didn't like, came along. The Samaritan saw the hurt man and felt sorry for him. But the Samaritan didn't just walk away. He went over to the hurt man and put soothing ointment on the cuts and scratches on his body and put bandages on them. Then, the Samaritan put the hurt man on his donkey and took him to a safe place called an inn. The Samaritan gave money to the innkeeper and said, "Take care of this man. If you spend more money for his care, I'll pay you the next time I'm here."

After telling this story, Jesus asked, "Who do you think was a good neighbor to the hurt man?"

The man replied, "The one who helped him."

Jesus said, "Yes, now go and do the same."

Main Point

In the Kingdom of Heaven we must love and care for everyone.

Take Action

1. When someone is sad, how can you help them feel better?
2. How do you feel when someone helps you?

The Lost Sheep

Scripture
Luke 15:1—7

Some religious leaders called Pharisees thought everyone should follow all the rules and act perfectly. They didn't like that Jesus spent time with people who did bad things. One day, they saw Jesus with these people and said, "Look! This man welcomes sinners and even eats with them!" But Jesus knew that God wants everyone to come to Him, so He told them the story of the Lost Sheep:

A man owned one hundred sheep. One day, one of the sheep wandered away from the flock and got lost. So, the man left the ninety-nine sheep in the care of someone else so that he could search for the one that was lost. When the man finally found the lost sheep, he was so happy that he placed it on his shoulders and carried it all the way home.

When the man got home, he asked his friends and neighbors to celebrate with him because he had found his lost sheep.

When people turn away from God, they are like a lost sheep. But when they return to God, everyone in Heaven is filled with joy.

Main Point

God loves you and He wants you to belong to Him.

Take Action

1. Pray and thank God that He doesn't want anyone to be lost.

2. Show others that they are valuable by being kind and loving like Jesus is to you. This way, others will know that Jesus loves them too.

The Lost Coin

Scripture
Luke 15:8—10

How do you feel when you find something that you lost? Jesus shared a story about a woman who had ten silver coins that were worth a lot of money. One day she lost one of the coins. She searched carefully all around her house until she found it. When she found the coin, she was so happy that she called her friends and neighbors to come over to celebrate with her.

Just like the woman rejoiced over finding one lost coin, God rejoices over each person that comes to believe in Him.

Main Point

Everyone is important to God. He wants us to turn from sin and come into His Kingdom.

Take Action

1. **How can you pray for someone who doesn't know about God's love?**
2. **How can you tell others about Jesus?**

The Lost Son

Scripture
Luke 15:11—32

Did you know that God's heart is full of compassion for His children? Jesus told a story to teach us about this kind of love:

A man had two sons. The younger son said to his father, "I want my money now. I don't want to wait until you are old." So the father divided his money between his sons. A few days later, the younger son packed his bags and went to a country far away. While he was there, he spent all the money.

After a while, the land was dry, and he could not find food to eat. The son got a job feeding pigs. He was so hungry that he wanted to eat the pigs' food, but no one gave him anything to eat.

Then he said to himself, "I'm dying of hunger. I will go home to my father and ask him to make me like one of his hired servants."

When he was almost home, his father saw him coming. His father was so happy to see him that he ran to his son and hugged him. The son was sorry that he had spent the money on foolish things. He told his father he didn't deserve to be called his son.

But the father told his servants to bring the best clothes in the house to put on his son and prepare a dinner party to celebrate.

Later, the older brother came home from work and wouldn't go inside the house when he heard the celebration for his brother. The older brother became jealous of his brother and angry with the father for celebrating the son who had wasted his money.

The father said, "We celebrate this happy day because your brother was lost, but now he is found."

Main Point **When people say they are sorry for turning away from God and ask Jesus to forgive them, He will welcome them into His Kingdom.**

Take Action

1. **Write or draw a letter to God, thanking Him for His love.**

2. **What's something nice you can do today to show someone you care about them?**

The Wise and Foolish Bridesmaids

Scripture
Matthew 25:1—13

No one knows when Jesus is coming back. That's why He wants us to be ready. Jesus shared this story to remind His friends to always be ready for when He comes back:

Ten bridesmaids were invited to a wedding. They took their oil lamps and went out to meet the bridegroom. Five of the bridesmaids were wise and brought extra oil for their lamps. But five of them were foolish and didn't bring extra oil.

It was getting late in the day, and the bridegroom had not arrived. So, the bridesmaids fell asleep.

At midnight, they woke up when they heard someone shouting, "The bridegroom is coming! Come and meet him!"

All the bridesmaids got up and prepared their lamps. Then the five foolish ones said to the wise, "Our lamps are going out. Please give us some of your oil." But the wise bridesmaids answered, "There is not enough oil for all of us. Go to a store and buy some for yourselves."

Can you imagine what happened next?

While the five foolish bridesmaids were away buying oil, the bridegroom arrived. Those who were ready went in with him to the wedding dinner. When the five foolish bridesmaids returned, they couldn't go inside because it was too late, and the door was locked.

Main Point

Jesus is the bridegroom, and He is coming back for all who believe in Him.

Take Action

1. How can you be ready to meet Jesus when He returns?
2. Say thank you to Jesus that He is coming back someday.

The Talents

Scripture
Matthew 25:14—30

Everything we have is a gift from God so that we can use it to help others. Jesus told this story about a man who wanted his servants to use what he gave them wisely:

One day a man went on a long trip to a faraway country. Before leaving, he called for his servants and gave them his money to take care of while he was away. He gave five bags of money to one servant, two bags of money to another, and one bag of money to another.

After a long time, the master returned from his trip and asked each servant what they did with his money. The servant who received five bags of money doubled it by working hard and making good choices. The servant who got two bags of money doubled his too!

The master gave both of them more important jobs because they took good care of his money.

The servant who got one bag of money said, "I dug a hole in the ground and hid your money because I was afraid that I would lose it. Here is your money back."

The master replied, "You are a bad and lazy servant! Why didn't you at least put my money in the bank so it could grow?"

Then the master ordered that the money be taken from this servant and given to the one with the ten bags of money. The master said, "Those who do well will be given more. But those who do nothing will have less."

Main Point

God gives everyone special talents and skills. He is pleased when we use them to honor Him and to help others.

Take Action

1. What talents or skills do you have? How can you use them to help others?
2. What are some good things that might happen if you work hard and try your best?

The Two Sons

Scripture
Matthew 21:28—32

Did you know that the way you act can show what's in your heart? Jesus told a story about a father and his two sons to help us understand.

A father had two sons. He said to the first son, "Son, go and work today in my garden." The son said, "I will not go." But later, the son knew that he made the wrong choice, and he was sorry. So, the son changed his mind and went to work in the garden as his father asked.

Then the father said to the second son, "Go and work today in my garden." The son said, "I will go." But the son did not work in the garden, even though he said he would.

Jesus asked the people, "Do you know which son did what was right?"

They answered, "It was the first son who did what was right."

Main Point

What we say and what we do matter, but what we do shows if we really mean it.

Take Action

1. Why is it important to keep a promise?
2. How can you show what's in your heart?

The Mean Farmers

Scripture
Matthew 21:33—44

Sometimes people are treated badly even when they do the right thing. Jesus told this story about a man who owned a garden and how he was treated poorly:

A man planted a garden with lots of grapes on some land he owned. The man went away on a trip, so he put some farmers in charge of the garden. He trusted the farmers to take good care of the land and the grapes.

When it was time to pick the grapes, the owner of the garden sent his workers to help the farmers pick the grapes. But the farmers were mean to the workers and threw stones at them.

The man who owned the garden sent more workers, and the farmers did the same to them. Finally, the man sent his son, thinking that they would treat him kindly. But when the farmers saw the son, they treated him worse than they treated the other workers.

Jesus told this story to the priests and leaders because He knew they wanted to kill Him. The priests and leaders understood that this story was about their plans to kill Jesus, the Son of God.

Main Point

Jesus is like the landowner's son. God sent Him to save us, but people treated him badly.

Take Action

1. Why do some people treat Jesus badly?
2. How should we treat Jesus, the Son of God?

The Fig Tree

Scripture
Matthew 24:32—35

Have you ever seen a fig tree? The places where Jesus taught had lots of fig trees. In His story about the fig tree, Jesus said that when new leaves begin to grow in spring, it means that summer is not far away.

In the same way, things will happen that show us Jesus is coming back soon. Jesus also said that a time will come when the world, earth, and sky will be wiped out, but His words will always be true. He will keep His promises, no matter what!

We must get ready for Jesus' return by loving God and showing love to others. Jesus could come back at any moment, just like He promised.

Main Point

We must be ready for Jesus' return.

Take Action

1. Give two reasons why you are excited that Jesus is coming back someday!
2. Why is waiting hard?

The King Will Judge All People

Scripture
Matthew 25:31—46

Do you know that Jesus is a king? Jesus helps us understand with this story:

At the end of time, Jesus will come again, and His angels will be with Him. King Jesus will sit on His heavenly throne. All the people of the world will gather in front of Him. Then, He will separate everyone into two groups, the people who followed Him and did what He said, and the people who didn't.

The people who listened to Jesus and obeyed His words will get to enjoy God's Kingdom, but others will not because they turned away from Him.

Jesus said He would know His followers if they were kind to others by giving food to people who were hungry, giving drinks to those who were thirsty, sharing clothes with people who needed them, and visiting those who were sick or in prison.

Jesus taught us to do good things for others just like in this story. What we do for others shows that we believe in Jesus and try to do the things He said.

Doing good things can't make you a Christian, but it shows that your life has changed because of Jesus.

Main Point If you love Jesus, you will show kindness to others.

Take Action
1. Why is it important to show love to others?
2. What are some ways that you can show kindness to others?

Let Your Light Shine

Scripture
Matthew 5:14—16

Many people followed Jesus wherever He went. One day, when He saw all the people coming, He went up on the mountainside and sat down. His friends came around Him, and He began to teach them.

Jesus told His friends that they were like a city built on a hill that everyone can see. He also said people don't hide a light under a bowl. They put the light on a table so it can shine brightly for everyone in the house to see. In the same way, Jesus said we should be like a light for other people. We should live so that they will see the good things we do and praise God who is in Heaven.

We should tell others about His Kingdom and how He forgives us for the things we do wrong. Don't be afraid to show and tell others that you love Jesus. Ask God to help you do what is right so that you can be a good example. That's how we are a light in the world. Shine bright for Jesus!

Main Point

Let your light shine so you can show and tell others that you love Jesus.

Take Action

1. What are two good things you can do to let your light shine?
2. Why should we shine brightly for Jesus?

The Wise and the Foolish Builders

Scripture
Matthew 7:24—27

Why is it important to make good choices? In this story that Jesus told, we can learn the difference between good choices and bad choices:

Jesus said that two men set out to build a house. One man was wise. He built his house on strong, solid ground. When the heavy rains came, and strong winds blew, his house did not fall down.

The other man was not so wise. He built his house on sand. When it rained hard and winds blew against the house, it fell with a big crash.

Jesus said that if we follow what He teaches, we are like the wise man who built his house on solid ground. When troubles come our way, He will help us to be strong.

Main Point

Jesus is the strong ground that we should build our lives on.

Take Action

1. How can you make good choices?
2. How does Jesus make you strong?

Fixing a Favorite Jacket

Scripture
Matthew 9:16

Jesus wanted His followers to understand that He came to give us a new way to live with God, so He told this story:

If someone has a hole in their favorite old jacket, they can't fix it by sewing a piece of cloth from a new shirt over the hole. Do you know why? Because, when they wash the jacket, the new piece of cloth will get smaller and fall off, making the hole even bigger! Then, not only does their jacket still have a hole in it, but their new shirt is also messed up!

In this story, the old jacket stands for the old way people used to live, like obeying lots of rules and trying to be perfect. The new cloth represents how Jesus teaches us a better way to live by loving God and being kind. Just like new cloth doesn't work well with old clothes, Jesus' teachings help us become better people and be more like Him.

Main Point **Jesus came to teach us a new way to live with God and understand His love.**

Take Action
1. **Show love by telling a family member one thing you like about them.**
2. **Draw a picture of something that reminds you of God's love.**

The Sower

Scripture
Matthew 13:3—23

One day, Jesus was sitting by the lake, and many people came to listen to Him. So, He got into a boat and sat down, while everyone stayed on the shore. Then Jesus told them this story:

A farmer went out to plant some seeds. While he scattered them across his field, some seeds fell on the side of the road, and birds came and ate them. Some seeds fell on the ground where there wasn't enough dirt. These seeds grew quickly because the ground wasn't deep. But when the hot sun came out, the plants dried up because their roots couldn't go deep enough into the ground to get water. Some other seeds fell among thorny weeds. The weeds grew up and choked the plants, making it hard for them to grow. But other seeds fell on good soil and grew into strong plants that produced a lot of fruit.

Our hearts are like soil that receives the seed of the Word of God. But how someone feels inside can affect how they listen and respond to the message. Here are four things that can happen when a person hears about the Kingdom of Heaven:

1. The person hears but doesn't understand the message. This means that the devil has caused him to forget the truth he heard about Heaven.
2. The person hears the message and quickly receives it with joy. But when trouble comes into his life and he is treated badly for believing the message, he turns away and stops believing.

3. The person hears the message but cares more about other things in the world. So, the message gets blocked and there is no good change in his life.
4. The person hears and understands God's word and follows it with the help of the Holy Spirit, our special Helper. Then this person shows love, joy, peace, and other good things in his life.

We get to decide what kind of soil our hearts will be.

Main Point

The teachings of Jesus can help us when we have hearts that are open and ready to listen.

Take Action

1. **Keep your mind on God by praying or listening to a Bible story every day.**
2. **Ask God to help you have a heart that listens to Him and obeys Him.**

The Mustard Seed

Scripture
Matthew 13:31—32

Did you know that something small can make a big difference? Jesus told this story to help us understand how that can happen:

The Kingdom of Heaven is like a tiny mustard seed that a man plants in the ground. Even though it's the smallest seed, it grows into one of the biggest plants in the garden. The plant becomes so big that birds come and make their nests in its branches.

You can't see the seed when it's in the ground, but when it grows into a big tree, it makes more seeds that will grow into more trees. God's Word can grow in you just like a seed. And when you share God's Word with others, it helps them grow too!

You might wonder, "How does a seed grow into a tree?" It needs water, sunlight, and someone to take care of it. In the same way, our faith in Jesus grows when we pray, listen to Bible stories, and spend time with others who tell us more about Jesus. Our faith starts small but can grow big and strong.

Jesus wants His Kingdom to grow too, by adding more people who believe in Him, follow His teachings, and grow in their faith. As more people believe in Jesus and grow in their own faith, God's Kingdom gets bigger and stronger.

So, the Kingdom of Heaven starts in you when you believe in Jesus. Then, it spreads to the whole world as you share what you believe with others. That's how God's Kingdom grows!

Main Point

Share what you believe about Jesus with others so that God's Kingdom will grow.

Take Action

1. **Pray and ask Jesus to help you learn more about Him.**
2. **What is something Jesus has done for you that you can share with others?**

The Net

Scripture
Matthew 13:47—50

Some of Jesus' followers were fishermen, so Jesus told this story to help them understand more about His Kingdom:

Jesus said the Kingdom of Heaven is like a fishing net that was let down into the ocean where fishermen scooped up different kinds of fish. When the net was full, the fishermen pulled the net to shore. They sat down and put the good fish in baskets and threw the bad fish away.

Jesus said that in a similar way, at the end of time, He will separate His followers from the people who do not believe in Him. People who believe in God, love Him, and do what He wants them to do will be with Him in Heaven forever. And the people who don't believe in God will live in a sad place away from Him.

Jesus wants everyone to choose to be in Heaven with Him!

Main Point

Jesus wants everyone to live with Him. He knows who loves Him and who doesn't.

Take Action

1. How can you be kind to someone today?
2. Pray and ask Jesus to help you make good choices today.

The Growing Seed

Scripture
Mark 4:26—29

Have you ever planted a seed and watched it grow into a plant or flower? Jesus said the Kingdom of God is like a farmer who plants a seed in the ground. The seed grows all through the night and day. It doesn't matter if the farmer is asleep or awake; the seed still grows. The seed grows into a plant that pops up out of the ground without any help. When the plant is all grown up, the farmer cuts it down and brings it inside to enjoy.

When we tell people about God and show kindness to others, we plant seeds in their hearts, just like a farmer plants seeds in the ground. The more they learn about Jesus, the more the seed in their heart will grow.

Just like it takes time for a seed to grow into a plant or flower, it also takes time for someone to grow in their friendship with God. When the right time comes, Jesus will bring everyone who trusts Him into God's Kingdom.

Main Point

It takes time to keep learning more about God.

Take Action

1. Spend time talking to God every day, like when you wake up or before bed.
2. Listen to Bible stories to learn more about God's love.

The Two Who Owed

Scripture
Luke 7:41—43

One time, Jesus went to eat at the house of a man named Simon. While they were eating, a woman came in and asked Jesus to forgive her. Simon didn't like this, so to help Simon understand why forgiveness is important, Jesus told this story:

Two men owed money to the same banker. One man owed 500 silver coins. The other man owed 50 silver coins. Neither of the men had money to pay the banker back. The banker forgave both of them and told them they didn't have to give him any money.

Both men were happy the banker didn't make them pay him back. But the man who owed the most, was the happiest.

God doesn't make people pay for their sins because Jesus paid for our sins when He died on the cross. People who are forgiven by God should be thankful and full of joy.

Main Point

God forgives our sins when we tell Him we are sorry, because Jesus paid for our sins when He died on the cross.

Take Action

1. Say a prayer thanking God for forgiving your sins.
2. How can you show Jesus that you're happy He forgives you?

The Friend at Midnight

Scripture
Luke 11:5—13

One night, after Jesus finished praying, one of His friends said to Him, "Lord, please teach us how to pray." Jesus then told this story to help them understand how to pray better.

A kind lady was surprised by friends who suddenly came to her house late at night. They were hungry after a long trip. The lady didn't have any food to give them, so, she went to her neighbor to ask for three loaves of bread. It was midnight, and her neighbor was in bed.

The neighbor didn't want to help because everyone in her house was sleeping. But the lady kept asking for bread to feed her friends until the neighbor finally got up and gave her the food she needed.

In the same way, Jesus says that we should not give up praying for what we need. We can keep asking God and trust Him because He loves us. God will always do what is best for us.

Main Point

Keep praying to God for what you need.

Take Action

1. Who can you pray for today?
2. How can you show your friends and neighbors that you care about them?

The Unfruitful Fig Tree

Scripture
Luke 13:6—9

God wants us to be part of His family, and we join His family when we believe in Jesus. Some people believe right away, but some people don't believe right away. God is patient and waits for people to come to Him. Jesus shared a story about a fig tree to teach us this lesson: A man had a fig tree planted in his garden. One day he came to the tree looking for fruit but became angry when there wasn't any. He said to his gardener, "What's wrong with this tree? For three years I've been looking for figs and I haven't found any. Cut it down! It's just taking up space."

The gardener replied, "Let's give it one more year. I'll take good care of it and give it extra plant food. If it doesn't grow figs next year, we can cut it down."

Just like the gardener was patient with the fig tree, God is patient and gives us time to become part of His family. But remember, it's important to use our time wisely and choose to be close to God now, while we have the chance.

Main Point

God is patient and gives us time to become part of His family.

Take Action

1. Ask God to help you show good things in your life, like being loving and patient.
2. What is one way you can show God that you are ready to be close to Him now?

The Wedding Dinner

Scripture
Luke 14:7—14

Do you know what it means to be humble? It means that you don't think of yourself as better than others. One day, when Jesus was at a wedding, He noticed that people were trying to sit in the best places at the table. So, He told them that people who try to make themselves look important will end up being humbled. But people who are humble will be honored.

Then Jesus said to the person in charge of the dinner, "When you have a dinner party, don't invite only your friends, family, or rich neighbors because they will give back to you by asking you to their house for dinner. Instead, invite people who are poor, blind, or cannot walk. You will be blessed because they cannot pay you back. God will reward you later."

In God's Kingdom, serving others is more important than being seen as great by other people.

Main Point

Be humble. Put others first before yourself.

Take Action

1. What can you give to someone who cannot give anything back to you?
2. How do you feel when you give to other people?

The Big Dinner Party

Scripture
Luke 14:16—24

Have you accepted God's invitation to be part of His Kingdom? It's a chance to be with Him, just like in this story that Jesus told:

A man planned a big dinner party for his son and invited many people to come. But all the people who were invited said they couldn't come. The man was upset and said to his servant, "Go into the streets of the city, and bring in the poor, the people who cannot walk, and the people who are blind. Go out to the roads and fences and invite them to my dinner party so my house will be full."

Just like the man in the story sent his servant into the streets to ask poor people to his dinner, God sent his Son, Jesus, to everyone in the whole world to tell them that His Kingdom has come and is ready for them.

The Kingdom of Heaven is open to all who want to be with God.

Main Point

God invites everyone to be part of His Kingdom, but we have to accept His invitation.

Take Action

1. Thank God that He invites you to be part of His Kingdom.
2. How can you accept His invitation?

Conclusion

Jesus is a King, and His Kingdom is called Heaven. Heaven is a wonderful place filled with never-ending love. Jesus told stories, called parables, to teach us about God's love and salvation, how He forgives us, and how He wants us to live.

Jesus wants everyone to be with Him forever, but He gives us a choice. He is patient and gives us time to choose, but the sooner you become part of God's family, the sooner you will know His love and experience His blessings. Will you choose to be part of His family now?

Jesus loves you!

About the Author

Deborah Ellison is a hobby gardener who finds joy in nurturing growth—whether in the garden where vibrant plants bloom or in the lives of others. With a master of arts degree in Christian education and over twenty years of teaching experience, she's passionate about cultivating minds and hearts in the knowledge of the Lord Jesus Christ.

About the Illustrator

Dave O'Connell studied at the Center for Creative Studies for four years in Detroit, Michigan. He has worked for Skidmore Studio Detroit for over thirty years as an illustrator and artist, creating art for many clients, including Chevy, Mazda, Ford, Michelin, US Postal, Carfax, Serta, and storyboards for Superbowl commercials. Dave enjoys bringing the clients' scripts to life and seeing them on TV.

He has taught art classes at CCS Detroit and Macomb College. He loves painting and using his art to speak at camps, men's groups, and church youth events.

Acknowledgments

This book exists because of the inspiration of Jesus Christ, who is my Savior and King. May He be forever praised!

Thank you to Patricia, Tanya, and Olivia for helping me realize that I was meant to write this book, and to Glennie for keeping me accountable so I could finish it.

I am grateful to my mom, Francina, who is my greatest cheerleader, as well as to my family and friends for their love and support. I also remember my dad, Talmage, who wanted everyone to know Jesus. His example of faith continues to inspire me.

Thank you, Shabaka and Nitasha, for introducing me to Kathy, who recommended EABooks Publishing services. You all helped to make this book possible.

Special thanks to my editor, Crystal, for her wisdom and guidance, and to my illustrator, Dave, for his creativity and passion for his work. The illustrations are better than I ever imagined! And thanks to Dawn for her excitement and support. You all played a big part in making this book what it is.

www.ingramcontent.com/pod-product-compliance
Lightning Source LLC
LaVergne TN
LVHW010027070426
835510LV00001B/18